635.9   Love, Gilly.
LOV
         Making the most of
         outdoor spaces.

DATE			

3/00

BAKER & TAYLOR

MAKING
THE MOST OF
OUTDOOR
SPACES

MAKING
THE MOST OF
OUTDOOR
SPACES

GILLY LOVE

RIZZOLI
NEW YORK

For Jane Weissman, director of Green Thumb, and for all the community gardeners of New York.

First published in the United States of America in 1999 by
RIZZOLI INTERNATIONAL PUBLICATIONS, INC.
300 Park Avenue South, New York, NY 10010

First published in Great Britain in1998 by
Conran Octopus Limited
37 Shelton Street
London WC2H 9HN

Text © 1998 Gilly Love
Design and layout copyright © 1998 Conran Octopus Limited

ISBN   0-8478-2135-8
LC   98-65892

Commissioning Editor   Denny Hemming
Project Editor   Rachel Hagan
Art Editor   Isabel de Cordova
Picture Research   Helen Fickling
Production   Amanda Sneddon
Illustrator   Sarah John
Indexer   Richard Bird

Printed in China

CONTENTS

Everyone has a different idea of how their outside room should look. Your personal vision will inevitably be influenced by the local climate, the house you live in and the lifestyle you lead. When designing your outdoor room, you will enjoy a freedom of choice rarely encountered in interior design, where function dictates so many of the decisions.

The legacy of experience and wisdom from past generations and cultures may also affect our choices. This outdoor room (left) incorporates many of the features that were popular in the ancient gardens of Persia, which were designed to provide a quiet and cool sanctuary from the searing desert heat. As in this garden, the ancient Persian gardens would have included shady places; water in square or rectangular pools (usually adorned with fountains to create humidity and soft sounds); and trees, shrubs and plants chosen for their beautiful flowers and aromatic foliage. However, plunge pools and outside showers would not have featured in those times – such modern amenities are ideal in a climate where, for most of the year, it is hot enough to take a dip in a pool warmed only by the sun, or to cool off under a cold shower.

INTRODUCTION

The exterior space surrounding a home has an important influence on the inside, too. Whether we connect our interiors to the outdoors by means of a garden or yard, a rooftop terrace or even a tiny balcony, we are making real contact with our environment, the natural world, and we are subtly blurring the boundaries between indoor and outdoor living.

Space and natural light are two of the most important ingredients of harmonious modern living. To ignore the relationship between indoors and the outside world is to produce a discordant home. And yet, outdoor rooms are often at the bottom of the list of design priorities when planning major renovations in new homes or redecorating current dwellings. The secret of successful interior design is to create a home that truly reflects its inhabitants' personalities, and this concept may be applied to exterior design, too. Everyone, whether green-fingered or not, can appreciate the delights of a quiet, sheltered spot where one can sit out in the open air and enjoy an early morning breakfast or a leisurely evening drink.

Making the Most of Outdoor Spaces is a practical and inspirational guide that takes you through the entire process of creating an outdoor room that is tailored to your individual preferences. It starts with advice on how to plan the room from the initial concept, with a wealth of practical ideas for prioritizing your requirements, and shows you how you can transform even the most awkward of spaces into a comfortable and attractive living area. An amazing variety of different spaces is featured, from shaded basement yards to lofty rooftops, tiny balconies to expansive terraces. There are design ideas for types of lighting, furniture, flooring and fencing materials, and innovative ideas on how best to decorate your outdoor room, not only through colour and texture but also by including ornamental water features, plant containers and storage space. Three real-life garden case studies illustrate how outdoor rooms can reflect the specific requirements of their creators.

As you progress through the book, and as your confidence grows, you will be inspired by pictures of successful outdoor rooms from all over the world, where designers have used, among other elements, colour, light, water and plants to create a unique space that has become one of the most important rooms in the home.

PLANNING

The process of planning your outside room is similar to designing an interior. You need to define your objectives and priorities and then decide how best to implement them to create an attractive yet practical design.

Once you have assessed your needs in terms of lifestyle and budget, you should aim to strike a careful balance between your ideal outdoor design and what you will be able to achieve in reality, given the location of your outdoor space and existing features or constraints.

SPATIAL AWARENESS

There are two completely separate aspects to this basement terrace (right): the view from above, where the abstract rounded shape of the square floor tiles creates the impression that they are floating above a sea of white, light-reflective stones; and the feeling of quiet contemplation that is gained from sitting at ground level surrounded by an evergreen screen of contrasting leaf shapes.

Similar paving and stones are used in a very different way in this urban back garden (centre), where the subtle kink in the stepping-stone path leads you in a romantic manner to the table for two. Without the sensuous curve in the paving, the path would rush you to its destination rather than encouraging you to stroll and linger.

The ambience of this outside space (far right) is obvious. Comfortable sun loungers, protected and sheltered by the wall of the house, face a beautiful view. All around the terrace are clusters of perfumed white roses among the trailing ivies, clematis, campanula and geraniums, which combine to create a colourful tapestry of harmonious tones.

ASSESSING SPACE

When planning any outdoor space it is best to follow the rhythm of the seasons. You may not feel inclined to go out into the garden or yard in autumn and early winter, but this is the best time to observe its structure and shape, as many trees and shrubs are dormant and have less foliage.

One of the major differences between indoor and outdoor rooms is that few external spaces exist in isolation from their surroundings. If you have an outlook that gives you pleasure, don't block it with fences or walls. Some spaces have a wonderful view: a mountain range, the sight of waves breaking on the shore, the outline of a beautiful building or the rows of chimneys on surrounding rooftops. Alternatively, you may have a space that lacks any privacy, where every activity can be viewed by your neighbours or

by people walking past. If necessary, or desired, erect sensitively chosen partitions in order to make this space your own. A tall trellis covered with aromatic climbers secludes an outside room from unwanted onlookers; a thick hedge makes a natural barrier and also provides a windbreak – this in turn may create a microclimate where you can grow tender plants that would otherwise suffer from a fierce prevailing wind. A high brick wall surrounding the perimeter of an outside space may offer excellent privacy and shelter but may feel oppressive when you are sitting outside; it might also present a dismal aspect when viewed from the windows. Planting evergreen climbers or using weatherproof paint to decorate the walls may help to solve this problem.

BEFORE YOU START

- Make a plan of your space and how it relates to the building in terms of access, architecture, boundaries, etc
- Look at other properties to see how they have used their outdoor space
- Observe any restrictions, eg, listed or historic building, conservation area, tree preservation orders
- Decide your requirements in order of priority, eg, vegetables, fruit trees, containers or flower beds, herbs, children's play area, water features
- List the existing features you want to retain, and those you want to replace
- Decide on the services to be installed, such as water source for irrigation, electricity for lighting and security
- List the problems to be solved, eg, lack of privacy, too much shade, protection from wind or sun
- Consider when you will use the room – all year round, evening, summer
- Decide what kind of room you want to create: a peaceful sanctuary, a low-maintenance garden, a jungle, a place for entertaining guests
- Decide on a budget and a timescale
- Compile a file of ideas for walls and paths, planting and colour schemes
- List the projects you can do yourself
- Get quotes and check references

PLANNING & PRIORITIES

Whatever time of year you decide to start planning your outside room, and whether you prefer to regard it as a room or as a garden, be realistic and honest with yourself. If you hate gardening, don't create a space that requires high maintenance; if you love lawns but are not interested in flowers, turf the space and make it a celebration of grass. If you adore camellias but have an alkaline soil, invest in some large planters that can be filled with ericaceous compost. If you are unsure about what to plant, seek expert advice. A useful tip is to observe what is growing on your neighbours' property, as similar plants are likely to do well on yours. If your home faces north and you live in a cool climate with a high rainfall but want to enjoy your outside space all year round, a conservatory added to the back or side of your house may be the best option.

Unlike interiors, which can be transformed in weeks, outdoor rooms take time to mature and are affected by elements beyond your control – sun, wind, frost and rain. These unpredictable elements make it more difficult to plan, as the seasons do not always progress as you expect them to, but they do occasionally provide unexpected delights – an early spring, for example, or an Indian summer, with plants flowering more often or more profusely than usual.

You might want to retain, or need to improve, existing features. Mature trees can be pruned to improve their shape, and even sizeable shrubs can be moved to improve the framework of a planting scheme. However, if you are planning to plant or remove a tree, seek expert advice because many trees are under preservation orders, while the wrong tree in the wrong place can block drains and sewers or severely damage the foundations of a building.

If you want to make your outdoor room look larger, you can use visual tricks. Just as a pale carpet can make a room appear bigger, a small garden or yard covered with light stone gravel visually increases the horizontal dimensions. If you want to make your space a haven for wildlife, plant some evergreen climbers. A range of plants with solid or variegated leaves intertwined with those bearing flowers, fruits or berries will provide seasonal interest, too. Similarly, if the view of the house from the outside is less than attractive, some well-chosen climbers can soften and

INSIDE OUT

This outside room (far left) has an unrestricted open view of the garden and is protected from any rain or wind. The lack of natural light has been turned into an advantage by illuminating the space with the romantic glow of candles held in candelabra and wall sconces made from robust twisted metal. White-painted brick walls and a large mirror reflect daylight and make the room appear lighter. A timber post supports the roof beam and acts as a prop for a scented climbing rose which brings the garden into the room.

Small internal courtyards like this one (left) should harmonize with the surrounding buildings if the transition from one to the other is to be smooth. In this case, the white paintwork and interior furnishings are echoed outside with white garden furniture and flowers and the extensive use of silver-grey foliage. The external brick paving is co-ordinated to blend with the stained wooden floor and the muted blue and cream rug inside.

TABLE TALK

At the height of summer it is a welcome relief to escape from the sun and find somewhere cool. This seating area (right) has been meticulously positioned to provide a dining area that can be both sunny and shady. A natural parasol of climbing shrubs has covered the roof of a metal-frame arbour; the leaves create gentle dappled shade, yet it is still possible to sit at the table in the sunshine if you wish. At night, the table is illuminated by a central light with a green metal shade that is virtually undetectable in daytime.

At the planning stage, you should consider how your outside room will look during the winter when it will be clearly visible from the house. Arching evergreen bamboos (far right) make a striking contrast to deciduous shrubs; the soft brown tones blend sympathetically with the furniture and the woven willow parasol. Untreated wood will be affected by sharp frost and rain and will eventually disintegrate, but the silvery bleached effect is very attractive. A huge stone planter can be expensive but it is a worthwhile investment – it looks impressive both as a piece of winter sculpture or when brimming with plants in the summer.

disguise ugly architecture and can also be trained to surround rather than obscure the view of the garden from windows. Contrary to popular belief, climbers will not harm mortar, etc., unless the wall is ancient. Scented climbers can also give additional pleasure in summer when the windows are open.

If you plan to tackle any structural work, such as laying paths, constructing ponds or walls, employ a specialist company that has the equipment and knowledge to do the job properly, otherwise you may encounter unforseen problems halfway through the project. Bear in mind that if structural works are contemplated, it can take months to accumulate comparative quotes from builders and landscapers. Also, if your property is historic or located in a conservation area, plans may need approval before you begin, and it can take some time to obtain building permits from local authorities.

There are other aspects to consider when planning outside rooms, and one that needs immediate priority is security. An outside room may make a home vulnerable to unwanted visitors, and it is wise to include the outside at the same time that you review your security inside. Outdoor lighting triggered by movement can be very reassuring, and treating drainpipes with special paint deters intruders from gaining access to upper windows. Some security provisions can be decorative – plants, for example, may be used to repel intruders: varieties of pyracantha or berberis have such thick foliage and evil thorns that if they are planted against a wall few intruders will want to climb down them; varieties of shrub rose can be grown as a dense hedge with beautiful flowers and stunning hips as well as masses of the most vicious thorns.

A well-designed, well-constructed garden or yard should look good and function well even when it is devoid of any planting – the living elements should be regarded as the icing on the cake. The best paving, trellising or walling materials, constructed with care and skill, will last a lifetime and longer and will form the framework in which shrubs and plants are the furnishings. Invest in the highest quality materials and plants you can afford and they will improve with age and bear up well under any climatic conditions.

EXTRA SPACE

Small spaces demand bold solutions for the most effective results. It may not be immediately obvious where you should focus your attention, so think laterally. A front garden or yard, a rooftop terrace or small conservatory may well provide more potential than the space behind the house and offer a practical solution to the constraints of your available outside space. Consider all the possibilities before you make a decision and take a look to see how your neighbours have utilized their space.

WINDOW SPACES

Some of the most successful interiors are those where a design theme or style is carried through from one room to another, and you may extend this principle to include your outdoor room. In this contemporary home (right), clipped box in metal planters make a strong statement and fully exploit the limited space available. This distinctive detail is repeated on the other side of the house to maximize the effect.

Using individual planters is an unusual and attractive alternative to window boxes: the well-manicured spheres of box provide a constant display, and the plants in the small terracotta pots can be changed from one season to another. Also, if one specimen dies, it is easy to replace without disturbing any of the other plants.

The style and proportions of window boxes or planters should be sympathetic to the size of the windows. Choose designs that make a strong impact and be consistent by using the same style for all the windows on one façade. Even economical plastic window boxes can be made to look expensive and sophisticated with a coat of paint that matches the woodwork or the colour of the bricks.

The space outside your home often gives visitors their first and lasting impression of where you live. No matter how small or awkward this area is, you should be able to exploit its positive features and transform it into an attractive and functional addition to your interior living space. Thus, the gloomiest basement can become a riot of colour through the introduction of hanging baskets; the dingiest side alley can be brought to life with a touch of light-coloured paint; and the front entrance to your home – so often neglected or perceived as useless and ignored – can become a useful extra living or dining room.

If the front garden or yard is in a secluded location or well set back from the street it may feel comfortable to sit out in, but while it can be pleasurable to have lunch on the pavement front of a café or restaurant, it is somehow less relaxed to set up an al-fresco meal only feet from the curbside and in full view of passers-by. But if the front of the house provides the sunniest aspect, it may be possible to create a small dining area by surrounding the perimeter with a fence or hedge that is trimmed to about shoulder height. In this way, people may be visible from the street when you are standing, but will disappear from view when you take your seat. Any furniture will need to be transported to and from the house, of course, unless it is in some way anchored to the ground, since the front garden or yard is usually open to the public for deliveries and collections when you are not at home.

Dustbins or refuse bins are not the most attractive objects, but if the front of the house is the most convenient place for them a well-constructed shelter will conceal them from view. If space permits, you could even construct a lock-up cupboard to store bicycles or a baby's pushchair, which saves bringing these things into the house where they usually clutter up the hall. Alternatively, the entrances of many houses are improved by the addition of an enclosed porch. This provides a small room for storing equipment, hanging coats and keeping outdoor shoes and boots, and it also forms a double barrier between the home and outdoors and may make a considerable difference to the insulation of the house – invaluable if the front of your property faces north.

Many urban front gardens or yards are just big enough to accommodate a car. If such a project is envisaged, you should seek professional advice, as the additional weight will probably necessitate special paving.

BASEMENT SPACE

Many city homes and apartments have a tiny front basement below street level and this may well be your only available outside space. This Greek courtyard offers some useful inspiration. It is very small, and with this in mind the pots and planters have been deliberately chosen for their tall, narrow shapes so that they take up little space; similarly, the plants growing in them have been selected for their upright rather than bushy habits.

The fig tree growing here provides shade, but an alternative choice in a town basement might be an evergreen tree – this will give some privacy as its canopy grows to form a natural screen from passers-by. A similar effect could be achieved by training fast-growing evergreen ivies up and across metal supports fixed from wall to wall. If the bars are sturdy enough, they could also be used as brackets for hanging baskets which, in summer, you can fill with trailing annuals such as lobelia, helichrysum and cascading petunias.

In this basement, all the pots have their own drip tray – a useful labour-saving way of keeping the floor clean and free from water and muddy patches, which in a shady spot would not dry as quickly as on a sunny terrace.

ROOM WITH A VIEW

When an outdoor room directly adjoins a house the transition between one and the other will be smoother and more harmonious if the two connecting rooms are planned and designed together.

The outlook from these floor-to-ceiling windows is visually pleasing because the lines of the adjustable wooden blinds are repeated in the lines of the mortar on the brick wall that faces them. The outside room looks larger than it actually is, because of the way the wooden decking has been laid at right angles to the bricks and slats of the blinds. This clever visual trick is echoed in the style of the furniture which, even though it is made from a darker wood, harmonizes with the walls and floor.

Creamy-white canvas awnings, resembling the sails of a boat, are suspended from fine wires; they soften the straight edges of the room and provide strategically positioned shade.

Bay laurel will thrive in a sheltered spot like this; for best results, grow them in tubs or large planters. You can easily retain the spherical shapes of these standard trees by pruning them every summer.

Some city houses, or those divided into two or three apartments, have an entrance at ground level with an open space in the basement that may receive very little natural light. Painting the walls white or in a pale colour, and laying a pale-coloured floor, will help to brighten up the area and create an illusion of space and light.

Although the level of natural light is low in basement spaces, the close proximity of the surrounding walls does offer the advantage of shelter from the damaging effects of wind and frost. It may therefore be possible to grow varieties of plants and shrubs in your basement area that would normally only flourish indoors. Ivies and other climbers like partial-to-deep shade, and would grow quite happily in a dark basement-level yard.

Hanging baskets filled with trailing plants and suspended midway into the basement offer a welcome splash of colour and, if positioned carefully, will not obscure any of the light to basement-level windows.

If light is not an issue, outdoor areas below ground level may be made completely private by constructing an overhead framework and training fast-growing climbers up the walls to create a canopy of green leaves. Once the plants are mature, you will be virtually invisible to passers-by and, if you install a series of tiny outdoor lights among the foliage, you will have an attractive and secluded spot for informal summer suppers.

A narrow corridor at the side of a house, often linking front and back gardens or yards, gives practical access but presents a difficult shape for utilizing as a useful living space. Also, it may well have restricted light if it is flanked by the wall of the house and a high boundary fence. To link the interior of the house with the outside it may be possible to knock through part of the external wall and install a pair of French doors or even a small conservatory, which will help to give the interior room or hallway access to natural daylight. However, you should bear in mind that any structural changes, particularly those involving external walls, may require official permission before you begin to alter the outside appearance of the property.

Once you have opened up an exterior wall of the house, this could have a dramatic effect on the way you perceive the related interior rooms. A room previously used only at night because of its lack of natural light may now become the most popular living space during the day.

LIGHT & SHADE

Strong natural light and shade are used to great effect in this outside room, where the lattice structure of the ceiling creates diagonal and rectangular patterns on the walls and ground. Three contrasting types of stone flooring have been laid in geometric shapes and reveal startlingly different textures in the light. The Swiss cheese plant has natural perforations in its leaves, which allows light to penetrate to the lower fronds.

Many deciduous trees are suitable for a small garden, yard, or outside room: they will give pleasant natural shade in summer and punctuate the changing seasons with fresh buds in spring and mellow red foliage in autumn.

Some decorative perennials, such as hosta, adore partial-to-deep shade and a rich, well-drained soil. If you grow hosta in pots (right), you can move them easily and also minimize any potential damage from slugs and snails.

The walls in this courtyard are high enough to provide privacy but do not completely obscure the fine woodland view beyond. By contrast, the town courtyard (far right) is more introverted in its design and creates an atmosphere of seclusion and privacy. Although most of the planting is green, the variation of leaf shapes and colours prevents the garden from looking monotonous. At ground level, the borders have an informal appearance, but the carefully curved shapes created by the gravelled area are clearly visible from the upper windows, as are the changes in height and form. Fragrant herbs and lavender are planted close to the paths, and a pot of sweet-smelling nicotiana is placed just outside the balcony door.

COURTYARDS

By far the most common outside room in city homes is the courtyard or backyard. These urban spaces are usually extremely small, with the advantage that they don't cost a fortune to design and furnish. When they are linked to interior rooms by means of full-length glass doors you can make the transition more fluid by continuing the interior colour scheme outside. A pale or natural-coloured carpet is visually linked by laying cream-coloured York stone and it may be possible to use exactly the same flooring material, such as tiles, provided they are frostproof.

As sitting and eating can take up most of the space in a small courtyard, it may be wise to confine your gardening to containers. Pots and planters may be hooked onto wall brackets, clustered on steps and elevated on tiered wooden staging or decorative metal stands to give vertical interest and avoid excessive congestion at ground level.

REST & RELAXATION

In countries where summer may extend up to five or even six months of the year, houses are built with outside living in mind. For centuries, free-standing pergolas or wooden lean-to structures have been used to span walkways and provide welcome shade in the heat of the day. Variations in the styles of these canopies are endless, but ideally they should be designed to harmonize with the proportions and architectural style of your house.

This Mediterranean country house has thick, white-washed walls and a pergola that is solidly built to withstand the rigours of time. A substantial structure is essential if you intend to grow climbing plants up and over it. Apart from the very fragile stems of some clematis, most climbers produce dense and heavy foliage and twining branches which will cause a flimsy structure to collapse.

Softwoods are commonly used for pergolas, but before construction the timber should be treated to protect it from harmful pests and diseases. This does not prevent the use of decorative paints or stains, many of which have preservative qualities, too.

TERRACES & VERANDAHS

In many homes, there is a paved area at the back of the house offering the potential for creating an additional room. The way you mark the transition between house and garden or yard is one of the most crucial aspects of the design of your terrace or verandah – easy access is essential if the outdoors is to be integrated successfully with the indoor spaces. Full-length glass doors combine function with visual effect and will enable you to enjoy the garden from the inside all year round; your outside space will feel like part of your home whatever the weather.

If you have a terrace which is south-facing and sheltered from the wind it may become very overheated in summer. A simple loggia (roofed gallery) construction could offer the desired amount of cooling shade for both people and plants; if the room is used most of the year this will be a viable investment. A cheaper option would be to construct a very basic frame which can be covered with a canvas awning; this will act as a sunshade as well as providing protection from the occasional shower of rain.

A garden umbrella could offer sufficient shade if you intend to enjoy leisurely lunches on the terrace. Many designs of outside tables can accommodate an umbrella in a central hole; base weights are an optional extra but are necessary when a ground spike is not appropriate, for even on the most sheltered terrace a sudden gust of wind could make an insufficiently tethered umbrella lift off into space. It is also wise to choose an umbrella with a diameter that generously extends beyond the dimensions of your table, as it is impossible to relax when the sun is burning your neck or there is a blinding glare reflected up from the table.

Wooden pergolas provide height and structure in a garden or yard and, when covered with leaves, make a shady and private place to sit. It can take several years for flowering climbers like wisteria and clematis to achieve this effect, but climbing annuals such as sweet peas and runner beans make useful and attractive stand-ins until the perennials have established themselves.

This balcony (right) is little more than a large metal shelf supported by triangular brackets at each side and confined by a simple railing. It is not even big enough for a single chair, which has to be placed half in and half out of the room. But it is possible to sit and feel as if you are actually outside in the garden.

The interior living room benefits considerably from the cool air that flows through the French windows, as well as from the close proximity of the container plants at the balcony's edge.

The garden itself is tiny and most of the available space is devoted to the cultivation of flowers and plants in raised beds around a gravelled terrace. Climbing plants are trained up both sides of the balcony; the wisteria should be pruned in late summer to keep it in good shape.

This garden requires regular, almost daily, maintenance to keep it looking perfect all year round; the comfortable chair on the balcony is therefore perfectly positioned for the gardener to sit and admire the view at the end of a hard day's gardening.

BALCONIES

In countries where daily hot sun is predictable for most of the year, the vernacular architecture has thick walls and wooden shutters to ensure cool and dark interiors, and balconies are constructed at every available window.

The balcony can be the most versatile part of the home. For generations, southern Europeans have eaten, cooked, thrown parties, dried the daily wash and chatted to neighbours across the way and in the street below, all from their balconies. These very special inside-outside rooms also have romantic connotations, thanks largely to the tragedies of Romeo and Juliet and Cyrano de Bergerac.

A popular feature of many apartment blocks, both new ones and those converted from former commercial buildings, is the 'Juliet balcony' – full-length windows with waist-high railings, which open into the interior. While there is no actual outside space, this feature creates the feeling of being in closer contact with the outside world, balancing the need for being outdoors with the privacy and security that an elevated apartment provides. With ingenious planning it may be possible to accommodate both plants and people on these tiny balconies, by restricting the use of containers to the vertical surfaces. Brackets on each side of the door would provide fixings for hanging baskets; window boxes could be attached to the railings surrounding the balcony on the inside or outside.

Older buildings with balconies may not have been designed to carry the weight of numerous heavy containers, and their weight-bearing capacity will need to be checked before large stone planters are installed. It is more practical to have several large containers on the balcony rather than lots of tiny pots. Plants grown in a deep planter can develop longer roots which stop them from wilting quite so quickly in hot weather.

Stone and terracotta pots have better water-retentive qualities but they may be too heavy for a balcony's structure. While plastic planters are considerably lighter they can be rather ugly. If you have to use them to keep the weight in check, conceal them behind more attractive containers or use a paint effect to simulate stone or even marble. A balcony can become a more integral part of the interior by painting pots in similar colours and choosing plants and flowers with harmonious tones that relate to the indoor room's decorative scheme.

IT'S A SNIP

Container gardening is the most practical gardening option on a balcony. This style of cultivation is one of the fastest-growing areas of the horticultural industry, and the choice of plants and pots expands every year.

Galvanized tin is a lightweight material and its silvery finish blends well with the painted brickwork on this city balcony (left). The containers are planted with box to make neat hedges and elegant topiary trees.

Box has been used for centuries to create ornate parterres and elaborate topiary and is currently enjoying star status as a fashionable plant of the nineties. It is a versatile and tactile shrub with small evergreen leaves that can be clipped into all manner of shapes, making it ideal for container gardening. On this balcony the tinware planters contain grey and white pebbles which stabilize the plants, retain soil moisture and keep the roots cool. Some of the larger shrubs are underplanted with silvery sage and rosemary which soften the formal topiary shapes. Lighting is subtle and low level, with tiny white lights woven between the containers and two halogen spotlights on a stake in one of the planters.

LOFTY IDEALS

I spent three years building and cultivating the roof terrace outside my attic bedroom (above). I wanted to create the effect of a country cottage garden in the middle of the city. In summer, the sweet peas and clematis completely cover the faded bamboo trellis around the perimeter; countless pots of sweet-smelling pelargoniums and aromatic herbs balance precariously on a three-tiered metal stand and around the edges of the stained timber decking.

ROOFTOPS

One outside room that is often completely separate from the rest of the home is the roof terrace, which can be designed as a total contrast to the interior. An outside room on the top of a building is at the mercy of the elements but it is also blessed with an unrestricted view of the sky; even if it is in the heart of a congested city it evokes a feeling of wide open spaces.

Rooftops specifically designed for outdoor living are built and supported to take the weight of people and pots, but many flat roofs, although they may provide the potential for an outside room, will need an additional

structural support to make them safe. Converting a flat roof into an outside room may also be subject to the restrictions of local planning regulations. Buildings that are listed or protected are often required to be preserved in their original form, and in the tightly packed buildings of a city landscape permission to construct a roof terrace may not be granted if it is perceived to compromise the privacy of people living in adjoining homes.

The height of the building on which the roof terrace sits will determine the type of microclimate this room will enjoy. Roof terraces are unlikely to be affected by the harmful effects of frost, unless the climate is extremely cold, and some familiar garden plants may behave very differently when exposed to extra daylight on a rooftop. Plants that would normally die off in a ground-level garden may well survive all through the winter and into the spring on a roof terrace. To ensure that your plants don't take over, leaving little or no space for people, stagger the heights of pots and trim plants regularly.

Rooftops are prone to the destructive effects of wind, and protecting plants and people should therefore be a priority at the design stage. Strong winds can permanently damage fleshy leaves and fragile flowers – constructing solid screens will only make matters worse by causing a downdraught on both sides. Wind-break netting or an open design of trellis are ideal solutions as they diffuse any wind to a more comfortable level. These can be virtually obscured in a few years if you plant hardy evergreen climbers in containers. But ensure that the containers are weighted as a tall plant in a plastic pot can easily be blown over. Alternatively, a hedge grown in a long trough can provide protection for more fragile plants.

SUNNY OUTLOOK

When a roof terrace is surrounded by high walls or a fence, it may be desirable to soften the hard edges with some foliage. On very small terraces this could be achieved by growing climbers at ground level up the side of the building until they eventually reach the top. On this southern Italian terrace, a wisteria has found its way to the roof. One of the most beautiful climbers, wisteria takes many years to reach full maturity and may be reluctant to flower in its infancy.

Trees of the citrus family are evergreen, and produce fragrant flowers and attractive, edible fruits, but unfortunately they cannot tolerate frost. On this rooftop, bathed in sunlight, lemon trees are flourishing in giant terracotta urns. Citrus trees need a fertile, well-drained soil and frequent watering during their growing season; these particular urns have been fitted with an inconspicuous irrigation system where the water is supplied by means of a thin plastic pipe. Irrigation systems like this may be connected to a timer switch so that watering can be programmed.

LINEAR PRECISION

An outside room used primarily for summer dining still looks attractive throughout the year when viewed from the kitchen balcony (far right). The outside world is virtually excluded by means of a well-constructed enclosure of trellis made from the same timber – Douglas fir – that is used for the staircase and the balcony decking.

An evergreen magnolia, grown in the narrow border behind the stone bench at one end, produces beautiful creamy-white flowers in late summer. The espaliered fig, trained on fine wires in a planting pocket at the edge of the balcony, is unlikely ever to produce edible fruits, but it remains in leaf for most of the year.

The atmosphere created by this secluded space is peaceful and calm when devoid of people, but it has been carefully designed to accommodate at least ten people around the refectory-style stone table (right), and it also provides enough space for a small party of friends and family to stand or sit and mingle in comfort.

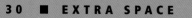

DINING ROOM

The architect John Pawson has a worldwide reputation for creating interiors that celebrate space and simplicity. Inspired by the minimalist architect Mies van der Rohe, and influenced by the four years he spent in Japan, John Pawson has applied his personal philosophy to the London home he shares with his family. Behind the two-storey Victorian redbrick house is a small garden, a typical example of those small overlooked spaces that back onto rows of other terraced houses.

Here, a unique private space has been created on two levels, linked together by means of a ladder staircase. This flight of steps has the strength of form typical of his work. The Douglas fir timber from which the stairs are constructed is also used on the 45cm- (18in-) wide boards of the balcony floor above, which are then continued through into the kitchen and the living room beyond. This outdoor room may seem modern and stark, but on closer inspection it is truly a garden for people.

LESS IS MORE

The plan below demonstrates how the relationship between the indoor and outdoor space is clearly defined in John Pawson's home, with the two areas in perfect proportion to each other.

The entrance is at the front of the building, and the kitchen and living areas are on the first floor. At the top of the stairs you pass through the kitchen and onto a balcony that overlooks the garden. Open wooden stairs take you down by the side of the house, where there are doors that connect the outside with the ground-floor rooms. The transition from one room to the other is effortless and appears seamless, because the same timber has been used for the internal floorboards, balcony decking, staircase and exterior trellis.

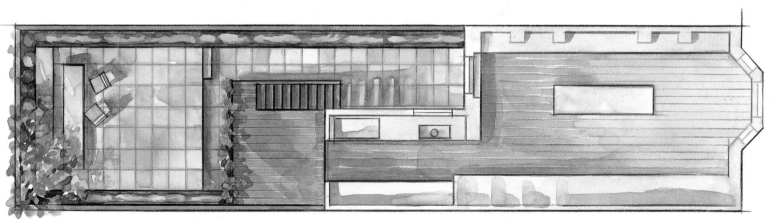

THE MOOD CHANGES

Even within the confines of a small garden or yard it is possible to create different moods, like theatre sets, provided that the overall appearance of the space is considered, and one area blends with another or is divided sufficiently so as not to cause a jarring effect.

Dramatic focal points can be very useful for distracting the eye from less attractive features. For instance, behind this blue-painted arbour covered with scented jasmine (right) is a rather ugly brick wall that marks the beginning of the next row of houses. However, you are not really aware of its dominance because your focus is drawn down to the arbour to the huge terracotta pot between two topiary box trees.

Around the lower terrace and outside her conservatory, Linda Burgess creates smaller-scale and more intimate cameos of seasonal arrangements. Ruby-red and lipstick-pink decorative cabbages contrast with the frilly heathers against a border of mauve, pink and white cockle shells (bottom right). This narrow flower bed has a permanent background of evergreen and variegated ivies, but the other elements are changed from one season to the next, according to the gardener's taste.

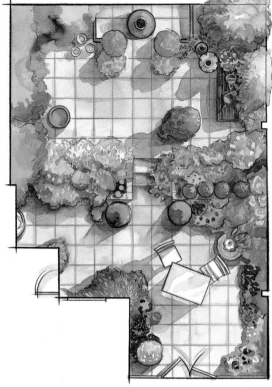

WORK STUDIO

Linda Burgess is a still-life photographer who makes full use of her garden as an extension of the conservatory and a daylight studio. Every available space is cultivated as a background canvas to provide natural environments for her distinctive photographs of flowers and plants . Much of the planting is in moveable containers, so that different scenes can be created in minutes, rather like a theatre set. The lower level of the garden is left clear for furniture and table settings for photographing food; when the occasion demands she imports several square metres of turf to produce an instant lawn.

DIVIDING SPACE

Changing the level of an outside space can make a significant difference to its overall appearance.

In Linda Burgess's town garden the concrete paving unifies what is in fact a small urban space at the back of a row of Victorian houses. The continuous flooring is made more interesting by its division into two terraces that are accessed by three steps.

On each side of these steps is a low retaining wall and two raised flower beds, which provide an option for dividing the space visually still further by planting tall plants and shrubs.

The flexibility of container planting makes it possible to create a living screen in summer, when the lower terrace is used frequently for outdoor entertaining, by moving taller pot-grown shrubs across the centre part of the upper terrace.

In autumn and winter, the division between the two terraces is not necessary and the low-level planting of lush green foliage, maintained by a computer-controlled irrigation system, is interspersed with the muted colours of button chrysanthemums, mauve asters and pale-pink heathers.

POOLS OF DELIGHT

In his garden, Kees Marcelis has used his architectural skills to produce a very functional and low-maintenance outdoor room. It has a delightfully light and playful appearance, created by water scattering down a glass roof, a jaunty metal gang plank used to bridge the narrow canal between the timber planking and gravel 'island', and the juxtaposition of different colours and textures.

Each view has been carefully considered – whether it be from the bedroom balcony or from the office behind the French windows. Paint colours and textures have been chosen deliberately to create different effects, depending on the time of day and the position of the sun.

Kees admits that he is no plantsman; he sought the advice of a landscape gardener before deciding on the heart-shaped leaves of catalpa trees and varieties of broad-leaved hosta and arching bamboos, which thrive in shadier areas. There is also a small plant glasshouse behind the pond, where tender plants may be overwintered and avoid wind or frost damage.

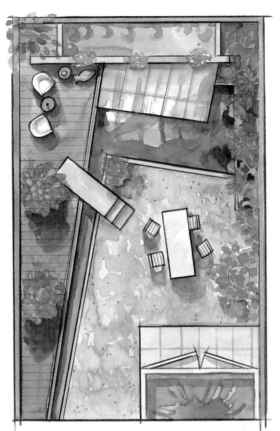

WATER PLAY

With the careful manipulation of space, Kees Marcelis, a Dutch interior architect, has made the small 13 x 8m (42 x 26ft) of his garden into a capacious room. Uninhibited by traditional designs, he tackled his outdoor space as enthusiastically as he would an interior space, using wooden planking, small stones, bold colours, diagonal shapes and running water. The result is impressive: the water runs down a transparent glass roof, falls into a reservoir below and is pumped along a narrow canal to repeat the process.

STYLE

The style you envisage for your outdoor room may actually be the starting point of your design process, particularly if you wish to create an unusual space – a formal area, for example, where all the elements are symmetrical.

Your choice of style may be driven by a desire to nurture a fine collection of aromatic herbs that provide a unique sensory experience. Or, you may wish to indulge a passion for brightly painted surfaces, exotic plants, handmade pots or church candles.

PERFECT SYMMETRY

The trees and shrubs in this hot garden have loose and spreading habits, yet the geometric symmetry of the hard surfaces gives it a classical appearance.

Formal gardens are often designed using a grid pattern, where the dimensions of squares, rectangles, circles or ellipses are all related. Here, a grid creates a harmonious balance between the width and height of the water feature, the square planting pockets and the stone paving stones.

The pump controlling the fountain may be adjusted to provide a soft gurgling spring or a gushing fountain; the base of the shallow pond is lined with a circular pattern of natural-coloured pebbles that give the impression of a ripple effect.

A well-weathered bench is centred at one end of the pool and provides a perfect place for contemplation, shaded from the rays of the midday sun.

Plants have been chosen for their ability to withstand continuous hot weather: spiky aloe vera grow in two rows of identical terracotta pots. The same style of container is used elsewhere in the garden to create an avenue of low foliage which links the house to the water garden.

FORMAL

The architectural styles of many urban buildings built before the twentieth century are notable for their formal features. Period themes visible on the outside are often continued in the interior; in fireplaces, for example. This formality may also be reflected in an outside room: through an authentic interpretation of a Victorian conservatory; in eighteenth-century Italian-style balconies and balustrades; or in ornate iron furniture influenced by designs found at the great châteaux of France.

The hard surfaces you choose for your outdoor room can produce a pleasing balance of simple clean lines in which geometry, proportion and symmetry are evident. This restrained and elegant atmosphere may well be appropriate to the architecture of the house or apartment. In other cases, you can create a classical ambience with stone statues as a focal point at the end of a terrace or path; or a pair of urn-shaped containers placed on plinths to either side of steps. Specialist companies produce authentic copies of classic eighteenth- and nineteenth-century designs using casts from original pieces.

Formality may also be achieved through restrained planting: trees grown as standards could be arranged in rows, avenues or at the four corners of a square to emphasize a geometrical layout. In smaller spaces, you can cultivate trees in Versailles tubs or other elegantly shaped planters. Neatly clipped hedges of box, yew or laurel make fine formal hedges, and the art of topiary is the ultimate way to create a formal effect. Choose slow-growing evergreens which you can then clip into spheres, pyramids, cones or multi-layered shapes.

RESTFUL HARMONY

One of the most satisfying projects you can undertake is the creation of a space where you can make time for yourself. It may be a quiet corner, with space to write and read, surrounded by treasured possessions – mementos of birthdays and holidays, pictures of friends and family – or it may be an entire room. Make that room an outside space and you will discover another world where nothing is rushed and nature dictates its own pace – you may even become addicted to the pleasures of gardening.

Acquiring even a small number of pots can provide enormous scope for growing a variety of seasonal plants. This very small courtyard outside a basement apartment is transformed into an intimate room: standard trees growing in pots rest in rustic baskets to create a rural effect; fat, natural beeswax candles are placed in terracotta plant pots; and urns and containers are filled with aromatic thymes and bay.

No digging or mowing is required here, just pruning and watering, but beware – container gardening is infectious, and once you gain confidence your pots are bound to multiply.

HOLISTIC

Many outdoor rooms are designed to be restful retreats from the stresses of everyday life – somewhere to enjoy the natural world in the privacy of your own home. The senses can be stimulated, soothed and nourished here.

Smell is a much-neglected sense that can be tantalized in an outside room by planting a variety of fragrant plants: narcissi in spring; wall-trained jasmine, honeysuckle, wisteria and the deliciously scented annuals – sweet peas and nicotiana – in summer. Pergolas and arbours could be covered with perfumed roses, or you could plant hedges of lavender, santolina and aromatic rosemary. Most scented plants exude their strongest scent from late afternoon; to appreciate it fully, seating needs to be close by.

Subtle lighting will add to the sensual experience; place candles in glass holders for a romantic flickering effect, or string tiny bulbs through the branches of trees and shrubs to illuminate a summer evening supper.

Sound can have an extremely relaxing effect; it could be present in the form of water in your outdoor room. A tiny spring gurgling up between large pebbles, or a continuous stream spouting from a wall-mounted fountain, will fit into the tiniest area. If space allows, a hot tub or plunge pool could provide the ultimate sensual experience. Cultivating specific shrubs such as buddleia, viburnum and cotoneaster will encourage the natural sounds of birdsong and humming bees. Windchimes can be a delight, but their volume is controlled by air movement, so avoid suspending them where they will catch a full wind; smaller chimes produce a more delicate sound, and those made from bamboo have the sweetest resonance.

Cater for your sense of taste by growing varieties of herbs that you will use frequently in the kitchen. Perennials like rosemary, sage, bay and thyme are easy to cultivate and add year-round flavour to your cooking. In summer, you could create your own salads from the mixed leaves of chervil, flat-leaf parsley and perpetual spinach.

Any plants in a holistic outside room should be grown organically if possible. Re-use bath and dishwashing water; conserve moisture by using a mulch made from shredded bark or prunings; choose plants that naturally deter aphid infestations by attracting natural predators. Organically grown vegetables not only taste sensational but can also look attractive when grown among flowers and herbs. Choose frilly-leaved lettuces, sculptural-looking artichokes and the ruby-red stems of chard.

As we stand on the brink of the twenty-first century, it is inevitable that we should look back over the last thousand years and anticipate the future in the context of what has already happened.

A positive and noticeable trend in gardening today is that gardeners are showing respect for the natural world by rearing plants organically and restricting the use of harmful pesticides.

A need to conserve valuable resources such as water has seen a rise in the popularity of drought-tolerant gardens, where plants are grown using a layer of gravel on the surface to help reduce moisture loss. In many countries, the driest years this century have occurred within the past ten years, and the long-term forecast is for more of the same.

These global climatic changes are making grasses an environmentally friendly addition to many gardens. In the United States, the planting of natural prairie grasses and other native American perennials is a growing trend that may change the current fashion for manicured green lawns that require the constant use of sprinklers.

The holistic garden is the garden of the future, where we can enjoy, preserve and respect our natural environment.

The bold use of open space – familiar in modern architecture – can seem rather intimidating. But when an architect has combined his own vision of a building with that of the natural world and they are in total harmony with each other, the results can be breathtaking (far right).

Although all the lines of this hill-top house are straight and all the corners are exact right angles, there is a distinct sensuality created by the perfectly proportioned pool, the bridge that spans it and the rectangular frame that captures the view of the city.

Clear blue water reflects the geometric shapes of the house, the stalks of upright bamboo and the spiky conifers which form a living boundary between the paving and the urban landscape. This outside room is an ideal example of an extrovert design where you are actively encouraged to look outwards.

The terrace (right), by contrast, has used clever visual devices to create an introverted space that keeps the eye within its boundaries. Artificial light is used to great effect, with the actual sources concealed. Bright halogen lamps simulate moonlight, and the corridor is illuminated by uplighters that make dramatic silhouettes of the tree's leaves.

MODERN

If you look at the designs of ancient Islamic gardens you will recognize many concepts that can be found in outdoor rooms today. The Persians perceived their gardens as a paradise on earth, a high-walled sanctuary in which the elements of water, perfume and shade were essential. Central springs or fountains provided soothing focal points and delightful sounds; water was channelled around the garden to irrigate the plants; avenues of trees were planted along the sides of waterways; flowers, usually fragrant roses, were grown in pots; and houses were kept cool through the construction of airy colonnades.

The significance of garden symbolism may have been lost down the centuries, but the spirit of gardens like those the Persians created is very much alive and finds its way into modern designs. Some larger spaces rely on computer-operated irrigation systems which can be programmed weeks in advance; solar lights powered by potent solar cells are charged by the sun during the day and turn on automatically at night; sophisticated advances in the production of glass and metal permit designers to produce transparent structures that appear to attach themselves seamlessly to buildings; and new materials, paints and stains provide durable and low-maintenance surfaces for furniture, fencing and flooring.

FANTASY

The design of some outdoor rooms might seem odd or unconventional, but for their owners they represent the realization of a fantasy space, which can either reflect or stand in complete contrast to the interior style.

Interior design and decoration are often limited by the constraints of certain basic facilities – cooking and washing equipment in a kitchen, for example, and beds and storage for clothes in a bedroom – but an outside room has no such requirements and its potential is therefore limitless. Allowing for the restrictions of the local climate and accessible space, you could perhaps indulge a passion for collecting exotic ferns, a skill for covering every surface with brightly coloured mosaics, a desire to recreate an authentic Elizabethan knot garden or a French potager, where herbs are grown with fruit and vegetables in neat and formal beds, or a conservatory with a constantly warm and humid environment in which to grow a tropical jungle of colourful exotic plants.

Your own style may emerge from one element: a love of scented flowers, a fondness for the hot-baked colours of Provence, or a yearning for the stillness and simplicity experienced in many oriental outside rooms, where raked gravel and sculptural shapes create a calming environment for quiet contemplation. Your fantasy might be influenced by a recollection from childhood – the sight of a field of bright-red poppies, or the smell of wallflowers. Or it could stem from the desire to recreate elements of your cultural and ethnic background, such as in the community gardens in New York, where tiny plots of shared spaces, alive with the colours, plants and buildings more reminiscent of southern Carolina, Puerto Rico and the Caribbean, nestle between the skyscrapers of the concrete jungle.

Simply copying ideas wholesale from another country may not be entirely successful, unless you can provide an identical climate and conditions, but a strong visual image may give birth to a host of imitable ideas that are truly original and personal.

Whatever style you choose, try to create an outdoor room that suits both the lifestyle you lead and the weather conditions the space is most likely to experience. It is possible to achieve any style and indulge any fantasy you desire, providing you give it the opportunity to flourish.

DESIGN IDEAS

Design features have to be well made and constructed from appropriate materials if they are to function satisfactorily and withstand the climatic changes in your outside room. There are myriad decisions to be made concerning the type of flooring, walls or fences to be installed, as well as the choice of furniture and lighting systems. Although you may consider and purchase these elements individually, the success of the final design will depend on how they work together in the outside space.

- Perfect paving is only as solid as its foundations – good ground preparation and expert application are essential
- Paving stones are attractive and hardwearing when you use real stone slabs but they can be expensive; secondhand stone is cheaper, as is reconstituted stone or concrete. Paved terraces need to be laid to provide a soakaway for drainage
- Bricks and tiles must be frostproof and preferably have a non-slip surface. These smaller-sized materials can be used to create curves and intricate patterns
- Gravel and pebbles benefit from being contained within a solid brick or timber edging. These small stones are relatively cheap and easy to lay as a veneer on solid, rammed hardcore and provide a natural and informal affinity with grassed areas
- Timber decking is an ideal surface to lay as a single platform over several levels of terraced or sloping ground. If well treated and maintained, timber is hardwearing, but it may become slippery when wet

UNDERFOOT

Outside flooring needs careful consideration before it is laid. The surface you select must be hardwearing and weatherproof, and you will probably also require some form of drainage. A paved stone terrace should fall away slightly from the building it adjoins in order to prevent rainwater pooling on its surface. A roof terrace should have a waterproof surface angled towards a central drain. However, these materials may be damaged if walked on so ideally you should install a suspended floor made from timber planks. Wooden decking can be laid perfectly flat because the rain will fall through the gaps between the boards. Softwoods make ideal decking, and it can be protected from harmful pests and diseases if you treat it before laying.

A gravel surface also allows the rain to drain through it, but it is not practical to lay gravel adjacent to a house as the small stones tend to stray inside on the soles of shoes and play havoc with vacuum cleaners. The laying of underfoot surfaces should ideally be scheduled with other works, such as installing electrical cables for lighting and irrigation systems; in conservatories, the flooring can also conceal the pipes for underfloor or perimeter heating.

UNDER YOUR FEET

A flight of otherwise rather gloomy concrete steps comes alive when the risers are painted in hot, bright colours (far left). These steps reflect the bright and clear sunlight.

Grass is one surface that needs constant maintenance, and mowing during the warmer months. This stepped lawn (centre, top) would be a nightmare to cut unless the treads were exactly double the width of the lawn mower.

Decorative patterns can be devised using a mixed media of paving that may create a 'rug' effect in the centre of a plain carpet of stone or brick (left, top). It is a good idea to restrict uneven surfaces to a small area since they are often uncomfortable to walk on.

A chequerboard design is made on a terrace (centre, bottom) by combining four square tiles with squares made from rounded stones that are a uniform shape and size. You can then choose to walk on the rough or the smooth.

The square slab is used again (left, bottom), but this time as a stepping-stone staircase where the severity of the slope is reduced by turning the direction of the steps every two or three slabs.

A wall may be used not only to mark the boundary of an outside space but also to divide an area in the same way that a decorative screen can be used to split interior spaces.

This staggered wall of glass bricks (right) provides a semi-transparent division between one part of the garden and the other and creates a sheltered seating area. A simple framework of steel scaffolding poles adds definition; eventually, the climbers planted in the gravel at the feet of these poles will grow up and over the structure to make a contemporary-looking arbour.

The reflective qualities of glass are used to great effect in this low wall (far right), where the bases of blue and green bottles are held together with rough mortar. Broken pieces of china or shards of earthenware could be used in a similar way.

A plain, rendered wall may be simply and economically decorated by pressing flat shells or smooth pebbles into its surface before the final layer of cement has set; you could then colour it very subtly with a wash of masonry paint.

WALLS

Some exterior walls or fences look better painted or stained, especially when they are brand new and attract unwanted attention. New buildings or boundary walls should be constructed from old bricks to match the colour and texture of existing masonry. If you choose to erect a fence, wood stains are available in a wide range of colours which are not just limited to timber tones. Many contain a preservative, which increases the longevity of the timber, and a colour pigment, which softens the harsh tones.

Even with high fences or walls, an outside room may still feel vulnerable to intruders. But your security arrangements can be both decorative and effective if you plant some 'defensive' shrubs or climbers that have bushy foliage and sharp thorns (see page 14).

Dark basement areas can benefit considerably from being painted white or another pale colour. A panel of brickwork painted lighter from the ground to about waist height can be a very effective way of visually lowering the height of a high brick wall. The lower band of colour may be linked to the wall above by fixing a section of trellis painted in the same colour. Painted surfaces provide year-round colour, which is desirable in winter when all but the evergreens have died down, or when you are waiting for climbing and creeping plants to grow.

SCREEN STARS

Walls may have decorative qualities yet still provide a protective boundary around an outside space.

This Mexican courtyard (left) feels completely safe and secure. It combines decorative railings with sturdily built walls, punctured by windows that are large enough to permit light to filter through but too small to compromise the room's security.

The metal curl detail on the railings is repeated to great effect on the arm and back rests of the dining chairs.

Another successful combination of materials is the solid-looking timber-framed window set into an equally solid stone wall (above), which provides a glimpse of the vegetable garden beyond.

IN THE SHADE

This enormous mosquito-net tent (above)
is so transportable it can be taken on
holiday, to the beach and on picnics,
as well as functioning as a protective
canopy for an outside dining table at
home. The double circular frame is made
from lightweight aluminium poles which
are slotted together; the tent is then
suspended at its apex from a suitable
branch or hook.

Another moveable canopy (right) is
made from an old and faded canvas sail
strung between the branches of shrubs.
The great advantage of this type of
lightweight shelter is that it is possible
to move it easily to a new location in a
garden or on a terrace as the position
of the sun changes during the day.

MOVEABLE FEATURES

Many design solutions have to have a degree of flexibility if they are to function well. The simplest example is the planter you choose for a tender plant that may need overwintering indoors. This container does not have to be frostproof but it should not weigh too much or it will be impossible to move once it has been filled with both plant and soil. Also, you should try to choose a planter which is not only appropriate for the decorative scheme outside but which will also complement the furnishings of the inside room where it will spend the winter months. An alternative solution is to fill containers that remain out of doors all year round with brightly coloured annuals that are disposable and can be replaced afresh the following summer.

If you have a greenhouse or a light and frost-free room, such as a conservatory, you can use this space for storing tender plants during the winter months. By keeping them in their pots, you can easily 'transplant' them, pot and all, into the ground in the summer and then dig them up and move them under cover again in autumn.

If your space allows, it may be worth considering investing in a multi-functional summer house. In the warmer months, it would provide an extra room for sitting and eating in, and a place for children to play; in winter it could become a vital storage room for vulnerable plants and for outdoor furniture and furnishings that would otherwise deteriorate in cold and wet weather.

The table you use for al-fresco meals in summer may double up as a bench which has several functions in a summer house: for shallow trays for germinating seeds in

early spring, for propagating cuttings taken from shrubs in the autumn, and for bringing on specially prepared bulbs in the winter. If you intend to store bulbs during the winter months, they should stand, off the ground and slightly apart, on dry sand or newspaper.

When there is absolutely no space outside for the winter storage of furniture and other outdoor accessories, you should make sure that every item is completely weatherproof, or that it will fold, roll or collapse flat so that it can be tucked away discreetly somewhere inside – under the stairs, for example, or behind a door.

UNDER COVER

In a temperate climate the chance to dine outside may occur only on rare occasions. It is important to consider how to make the most of these infrequent opportunities and to acquire the necessary furniture and sun shades. However, the designated space should also be contemplated in the winter, when summer foliage has died off and it is much more visible from the house.

This dining area (left) is an ingenious solution to the dilemma. A framework comprising rounded and square shapes will blend with the outlines of bare branches in winter, while in summer a canvas roof can be lashed to the structure to make an efficient parasol.

A treated timber table may be left outside permanently, with the metal folding-frame chairs brought out when required. These chairs are made more comfortable with the addition of removable canvas 'overcoats' that may also include a thin padded seat cushion.

Clematis and semi-evergreen honeysuckles are trained around the curved metal arches and are pruned regularly to discourage them from straying up any further, where they would be damaged by the addition of the canopy in the warmer months.

AL-FRESCO SUPPERS

If you are lucky enough to enjoy hot
days, and nights that are warm for
at least part of the year, this outside
kitchen (far right) is a practical idea.
A folding stove is fuelled by a refillable
gas cylinder; an enamel bath filled by
a hosepipe is used for washing dishes
which are then left to dry in the sun.

A permanent barbecue made from
preformed concrete (centre) makes an
elegant feature on this terrace, with
its clean lines and contrasting textures.

For al-fresco entertaining, table
decorations can be improvised from
trails of leaves and sprigs of herbs, and
illuminated by candles placed in a cheese
grater or simply secured by wooden
clothes-pegs (above).

OUTDOOR EATING

Food invariably tastes better when it is cooked outside. Fresh air sharpens the appetite, and charcoal cooking imparts a unique flavour that makes fresh fish, meat or vegetables taste simply delicious. Experienced barbecuers plan well in advance, as they know that it can often take some considerable time before the pile of charcoal has reached its optimum temperature and the coals are glowing hot enough to begin cooking.

The greatest deterrent to barbecue cooking is the wind. For safety, it is wise never to position any barbecue too close to buildings, wooden fences, plants or overhanging trees, which may get scorched.

Small metal hibachi or Japanese fire-box grills are cheap and portable. Even cheaper are disposable barbecues – self-contained packs comprising a heavy foil tray, charcoal and a wire grid. Kettle-style barbecues have a lid, which allows the charcoal to continue burning when closed and gives protection against a sudden downpour of rain. Light the charcoal with the recommended lighting fuel – never with petrol or paraffin (gasoline or kerosene), which are dangerous and can affect the flavour of the food. Charcoal is most safely extinguished with a fine water spray or by damping down with sand. Any remaining coal, once completely cold, can be dried and stored for future use.

Adding sprigs of thyme or rosemary to the coals gives additional flavour to food, as does marinating meat in spices, herbs and good quality oil – this also tenderizes cheaper cuts and helps to seal in the juices. If you are barbecuing fish, it is advisable to use a double-sided wire fish holder, which prevents the fish from falling apart as you turn it over. Potatoes and corn on the cob barbecue very well wrapped in foil and placed on the edge of burning embers; this way, the grill above is left free for cooking other vegetables, meat or fish.

Outdoor eating need not necessarily involve barbecuing; it may take the form of enjoying freshly brewed coffee and hot croissants for an al-fresco breakfast, or a lunchtime picnic of tasty dips and salads.

For you to truly enjoy eating outside, the experience should be informal, relaxed and easy. Meals eaten out of doors tend to be long affairs; seating should therefore be comfortable and the table may require shading with a canopy or parasol to protect both the diners and their food.

ONE ROOM OR TWO?

A room within a room has successfully been created on this capacious terrace, which includes many design ideas that could easily be replicated in your home on a less grand scale.

A black-painted tubular steel arbour defines the boundaries of the 'living room' and provides a frame for lines of fine wires to which climbing plants are trained to provide shade. Heavy fabrics with an eastern influence are draped over the frame for additional shade and shelter. The rich and sumptuous theme is continued in the choice of upholstery, scatter cushions and kelim rug. The sofas are raised on large bricks and covered with firm seat and back cushions with bolsters for arm rests. With their abundance of small scatter cushions, these sofas are designed for relaxed lounging, in the warmth of dappled shade during the day or in the soft glow of low-level candles at night.

This location evokes an exotic and tropical atmosphere, but such a setting could easily be recreated in a warm conservatory, which would provide a suitable climate for equatorial plants. You could even create a similar effect outside, as all the soft furnishings could be brought inside during winter.

FURNITURE

Most public outdoor seating is decidedly uncomfortable. An exception is the deckchair, the universally popular seat for outside rooms. Deckchairs are lightweight, collapsible, portable, easy to store, cheap and – most important of all – ideal for sitting or lounging. A basic deckchair can easily be customized by painting or staining the frame and changing the canvas to match any colour scheme.

Many popular seating designs started life outdoors but look equally good inside the home. Director's chairs, and other folding wooden and metal seats, can be transferred onto a balcony or terrace whenever the weather permits, avoiding the need to have separate indoor and outdoor

furniture. Traditional deckchairs and hammocks are unlikely to be incorporated into most interiors, but can be stored flat under a bed when not in use. Woven wicker and cane furniture blends perfectly in most outside rooms: Lloyd Loom chairs and sofas, designed in the 1930s, are a comfortable choice for conservatories or exteriors but they should not be left out in the rain. Constructed with a wooden frame, covered with woven fibres made from wire and covered with brown kraft paper, these designs are sprayed with a water-based lacquer in natural or painted colours. Originals can still be found in antique shops and modern versions are readily available. All-year-round outdoor furniture must be made from weatherproof materials, such as metal, stone or treated softwoods.

It is easy to forget the visual impact that strong sunlight can have on outside structures, where it can create the most fascinating shadow patterns. For instance, the trellis structure (right) surrounding a sunny seating area diffuses hot sun to a more comfortable degree and also produces subtle decoration in the light patterns on the wall. As a result of painting the wall a deep midnight blue, the white light makes a stronger contrast with it.

With careful positioning, artificial light, too, can create dramatic effects – when installed at the bottom of a pond, for example, or at the base of a tree. If you conceal lights in the undergrowth, they will sharply define the shapes of leaves and branches.

For sheer romanticism, you cannot go wrong with candlelight. Suspended from the gnarled horizontal branches of this mature frangipani tree (far right) are hurricane lamps. They emit a soft warm glow that lights up the table below and emphasizes the mottled texture of the tree's trunk and branches.

LIGHTING

Hot summer evenings spent sitting in your outdoor room can be greatly enhanced by installing some creative lighting. Installing several all-weather electrical sockets allows you to plug in lights whenever you need them. If you want to use lighting decoratively, outdoor Christmas-tree lights can look stunning when woven through the branches of a tree or around the stems of a potted plant; architectural-looking plants present a dramatic appearance and cast fascinating shadows on walls and floors when

their leaves are lit from beneath with spotlights; or entrances can be adorned with a string of small bulbs. Uplighters can be incorporated into flooring if they are fitted beneath reinforced glass floor tiles; this gives the impression that the surface is glowing.

Bulkhead lights have a bulb protected by a toughened glass shade, held in place by a close-fitting metal frame designed to withstand the impact of ocean waves lashing onto the deck of a boat. Readily available, they look effective bolted low down on the walls of roof gardens and terraces. Many light fittings designed for bathrooms are ideal for outside rooms as they are resistant to dew and rain. Lights charged by solar power are useful energy-saving devices, but since most of these fittings are functional and rather unattractive, you will need to position them carefully so that they emit effective lighting while remaining as inconspicuous as possible.

Parties and barbecues need more fantastic, attention-grabbing lighting. You might want to choose wrought-iron chandeliers filled with glass candle holders and suspended from tree branches or a pergola; tiny night lights in jam-jars strung with string from hanging-basket brackets; or candles placed in rows on the tops of walls, at the bottom of step risers and along the contours of a path. Garden flares, which are designed to withstand reasonable wind, will burn for hours; their wax is sometimes impregnated with a delicate scent that discourages mosquitoes and gnats. If you have a pond, you could make a flotilla of floating lotus-flower-shaped candles which gently flicker as they bob around on the water's surface.

DECORATION

One of the joys of decorating an outside room is the enormous range of tones and textures provided by plants, shrubs and landscaping materials.

Colour schemes are not static and can be changed from one season to another; water may be used decoratively to create tranquil pools or softly gurgling fountains; containers offer the potential to produce instant gardens, and may be chosen to complement or contrast with their planting; and even storage space can be made to look decorative.

Colours can affect our emotions and mood states. If you paint and decorate a room in one colour and have a single central light or window, there is a danger that it may appear dull or unimaginative. A garden, on the other hand, may contain only green plants, but it will rarely seem dull because the tones will change as the plants are exposed to different levels of light during the day.

Time and weather may mellow the colour of walls and flooring, and in this outdoor room (right) the result is a harmonious balance, complemented by the vine above with its luscious palette of greens, yellows and golden browns.

Organic greens may contrast with paintwork (far right), but here there is a balanced relationship between surfaces and materials – the squares of concrete paving match the colours of the bricks and mortar on the low wall, and the woven rush mat blends well with the split-cane screen. Some colours need contrast to make them come alive; in this room, the green tones benefit from the acid-yellow slats on the seats and the midnight-blue tiles of the table top.

COLOUR & TEXTURE

The design for a colour scheme for your outside room should be given as much thought as you would give the decoration of any inside room. Even though you already have a ceiling colour – the sky – it will vary constantly, from grey cloud to numerous shades of blue, depending on the weather. Before you begin, you need to familiarize yourself with the way your outside room looks in different lights so that you can select a palette of tones and textures that

produces a pleasing atmosphere whatever the weather or season. Simplicity is often the most successful solution – an outside space that relies on natural green will reveal a wealth of different shades. The tones of deciduous and evergreen leaves change constantly all through the year, as well as after rain and when covered in frost. A carefully considered combination of evergreen shrubs can create permanent shapes and layers of texture with added seasonal benefits of flowers and berries. If you add to these natural elements the contrasting surfaces of walls, floors and containers, you will achieve a rich and unique scheme.

Too many colours can result in a chaotic confusion that is tiring on the eye; another drawback is that they can make a small room appear even smaller. Colour and texture can, however, visually expand the dimensions of tiny outside spaces. Vertical structures, such as pergolas and arches, create height and provide another surface on which to add seasonal colour. A well-proportioned framework provides sculptural interest when covered in winter snow and frost; it will also give a burst of fresh spring colour if planted with an early-flowering clematis; this could then be followed by a summer-flowering scented climbing rose.

In hot climates white is used extensively to reflect the sun. However, just as an all-white interior with north-facing windows can feel very cold, so too can an outside space if it faces north. Nevertheless, white can be used to great effect by growing shrubs with white and green variegated leaves, seasonal planting with winter-flowering snowdrops, pure white tulips in spring and gloriously scented creamy nicotiana, jasmine and roses for summer.

USING COLOUR

- Understanding the basic principles of colour can be extremely useful when planning an outside room. All too often, gardens can become a frenetic muddle of colours and textures that resemble a bowl of canned fruit salad

- *Colour hues* are the pure colours that are arranged side by side on a spectrum. They can be used in harmony, eg, crimson, violet or blue with blue-green foliage, or scarlet, orange or yellow with yellow-green or variegated foliage

- *Colour contrast* is achieved when opposing colours of the spectrum are used together, eg, bright-yellow narcissi with deep-violet irises, blue delphiniums with orange marigolds

- *Colour tints* are colour hues mixed with white, resulting in a palette of the same colour which has different degrees of paleness

- *Colour shades* are like tints but they are mixed with black and vary in degrees of darkness

- *Colour tone* is the intensity of a colour, which changes depending on your proximity to it. Bright colours are best used close to a building; softer, receding colours are used to increase the feeling of distance

THE LAP OF LUXURY

Although it is generally considered to be a luxury, a swimming pool may be a highly desirable outdoor feature in hot climates if your outside space is not close to the ocean or a lake. Virtually the entire available space (right) is devoted to a pool.

A well-constructed swimming pool is an expensive purchase and should be planned and built by experts. It also needs continuous maintenance if it is to provide a clean and clear expanse of water to swim in. Water has to be pumped through a filtration system – if not continuously, then certainly for several hours a day. A careful balance of chemicals is also needed to keep the water clean and hygienic, particularly if young children are using it, though saltwater pools are gaining in popularity. The pool may also require heating if you intend to continue using it throughout the year.

Having a swimming pool could make you and your outside space very popular with family and friends in hot weather. If the pool is lit from beneath by lights fitted flush into the sides or on the bottom, you can enjoy the sensual pleasures of nighttime bathing.

WATER

The sound of running water trickling over stones or plopping onto pebbles creates a soothing atmosphere in outdoor rooms. Small fountains operated by tiny electric pumps can be fitted inside a glazed and frostproof terracotta pot; a pump installed behind a wall-mounted mask causes the water to gurgle out into a separate or integral reservoir and then pumps it back again to repeat the process. Any electric cables running to a fountain or pond should be installed at the same time as the floor surface so that the wires can be safely and aesthetically concealed from view.

A water feature such as a pond is a great attraction for wildlife and provides a safe home for fish and frogs if you cover the surface with netting to deter predators. Pools should ideally be located in an open and sunny position, where they will stay clean – avoid shady areas, particularly under trees where the pool will become blocked with fallen leaves. Installing a pump keeps the water moving; if a filter is incorporated within the system it could be fitted with an ultra-violet light which kills off unwanted algae.

Square, rectangular or other formal-shaped pools may be incorporated into the paving near the house, and their geometric lines will follow the angles of the building. Farther away, natural, rounded shapes will blend more easily with their surroundings. You will need thick rubber sheeting, similar to that used to make car tyres, as a long-lasting and watertight base for ponds; it should be laid on firm ground and protected by underfelt. This material will last for at least thirty years and is far preferable to cheaper preformed plastic liners.

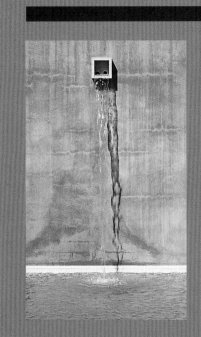

COOL CASCADES

Water is an extremely versatile element and can add many qualities to your outside space. A fountain can be used to produce energizing rushing sounds or a peaceful trickle – with a sophisticated pump you could even have a choice of both at the flick of a switch. On a smaller scale, water may trickle from a glazed pot into a pond, or gurgle from a wall-mounted ornament or pipe.

Still expanses of water may reflect a beautiful tree or the façade of a house, and at night the surface of a pool makes a beautiful mirror for reflecting the light of candles or lamps.

POTS OF INTEREST

The roof terrace of this modern home (right) has a clear and simple design that creates a feeling of open space with its glass and wooden-framed doors and the immaculate timber decking that is interrupted only by areas of pale, uniformly shaped pebbles.

Huge steel containers reflect the colours of their surroundings and are capacious enough to accommodate silver birch, evergreen grasses and pink-flowered thrift. Sympathetic combinations of plants may be grown together if the containers are on a grand scale, but individual plants can also be used to great effect in their own decorative pots (far right, top). Here, topiary box trees punctuate the wall of a chimney stack on an urban roof terrace. The trees are all uniform in shape, size and colour; variety is introduced through the terracotta pots that hold them, decorated with a colourful array of small mosaic tiles that stand out against the white-painted brickwork.

The simple terracotta pot remains one of the most popular and versatile containers (far right, bottom). These rounded, tub-shaped pots have a simple relief pattern which complements the cerise treads and risers on the steps.

CONTAINERS

One distinct advantage of container planting is that the type of soil available in your outside space never restricts your choices. Acid-loving azaleas can be grown in pots alongside troughs filled with the coarse grit that alpine plants prefer. A container garden can be created in the smallest space and in the short time it takes to go to a nursery and pot up the plants when you return home. This type of gardening gives you instant gratification, with the added benefit that if you decide to move house you can take your plants and pots with you.

If you plan to use heavy containers on a roof or balcony, distribute the weight evenly around the edge as this is the strongest part. If you intend to grow trees or shrubs, heavy containers are essential as the plants risk being blown over in strong winds. Replica bronze and lead planters are now made cheaply from resins – they are also frostproof. Solid wood planters tend to be heavy, but those made from fibreglass can look authentic when painted to contrast or co-ordinate with the colours of plants or other furniture.

Paint can transform harsh-looking plastic and it also lifts the darkness of cheap and readily available barrel halves. Over time, paint bleaches and fades but this will often enhance the appearance of the container. Terracotta pots can look rather startling when new; their very orange hue fades naturally with time, but the process can be speeded up if you give them a light coat of very diluted white water-based emulsion paint. If you prefer the look of moss and mould, try coating new pots with natural yoghurt and then leaving them somewhere cool and damp to encourage a bloom of green mould to develop.

WELL-ORGANIZED

Even the smallest garden, yard or tiny terrace, filled with container-grown plants, generates a quantity of tools and equipment which will need storage space as well as regular maintenance. A purpose-built shed is ideal and can be fitted with shelving, hooks and racks for storing all the essentials.

At the bottom of a town garden (right), a small structure has a sheltered position and is adorned with pots. The wall is covered with natural-coloured trellis which supports a shelving system and pot hangers that hold tender plants and seedlings in an elevated position away from ground frost.

Basic structures like this one (centre) do not have to be expensive, and if you give them several coats of colourful wood stain they can look highly decorative. Tools are hung on hooks outside in summer for easy access, and a basket is suspended near the door for convenient access to smaller hand tools.

A potting-up bench, especially one with a water supply, can be invaluable. A kitchen sink and drainer (far right) has been incorporated into a custom-made bench – the insulated pipes run directly into the shed to prevent them from freezing up in winter.

STORAGE

In most outdoor rooms there is very little space for storage because every corner has been utilized as part of the decorative scheme. Ingenious solutions are required if you have to store equipment, tools or furniture outside. The constraints on available storage space may influence your choice of seating, leading you to select chairs and tables that can be left outside permanently, or ones that fold completely flat and can be stashed behind a wardrobe or in a closet. Garden umbrellas are often bulky and, as a result, can be difficult to store successfully – you may want to consider an awning or canopy as a more feasible alternative. Ideally, some sort of storage should be incorporated into the design of an outside room at the earliest planning

stages. A raised terrace could be constructed to include a small underground haven for spare pots or bags of soil and compost; a bench could double up as a large watertight trunk, with space inside for tools and fertilizers or pots and candle holders. If the box contains poisonous materials, it should be secured with a padlock. A huge urn makes a wonderful piece of outside decoration and could also house equipment if covered with a waterproof lid.

No keen gardener would be without their greenhouse, and the modern aluminium frame structures provide the flexibility to create either a free-standing or a lean-to design. A well-organized greenhouse will give you the space to store equipment, materials and raise plants. Hanging baskets are also useful in a greenhouse, providing an off-the-floor space for germinating seeds.

STORAGE CHECKLIST

■ **Outdoor furniture** – Use a rust inhibitor on metal and lubricate hinges, springs and rivets

■ **Pushchairs and bicycles** – Allow enough room for easy access to equipment that is needed on a regular basis

■ **Dustbins or refuse bins** – A covered shelter will hide these unsightly items and protect them from the elements and their contents from scavengers

■ **Garden tools: spades, forks** – Keep clean and dry. Larger hand tools can be hung on a rack; prevent rust by plunging the metal head into a bucket filled with sand mixed with a little oil

■ **Garden tools: secateurs, shears** – Clean blades with wire wool (steel wool) and warm water; sharpen regularly and use an oily rag to lubricate metal parts

■ **Power equipment: lawn mower** – Needs professional servicing once a year; check cables for wear and tear

■ **Organic materials: compost, mulches** – Keep in tough polythene bags, sealed to retain their moisture

■ **Fertilizers: granular and foliar feeds** – Always store somewhere cool and dry, and preferably dark. Ensure that all containers are tightly closed and out of the reach of children or animals

SUN ROOMS

Gardens are for people. With that thought in mind, you may desire a special sun room. This could take the form of a separate summer house, used primarily in warm weather, or you may decide that a conservatory makes more of your home and creates a delightful transition between inside and outdoors.

The microclimate produced inside a conservatory will make you feel closer to the natural world and may even allow the cultivating of home-grown fruit, vegetables and semi-tropical plants.

A sun room, if positioned carefully, can provide shelter and shade from the fierce midday rays but be flooded with more gentle light at the end of the day.

This eastern-influenced entrance (right) commands a view of the house while creating a dramatic focal point at the end of a walkway.

For sun rooms that are occupied all year round, it is essential to have good ventilation. The doors to this modern conservatory (far right) fold back on themselves completely to encourage cool air to flow into the house. Split-cane blinds control the amount of sunlight entering the room, and pots and planters filled with evergreen shrubs provide additional shade and privacy. Similar pots line the glass walls inside the house and promote a feeling of continuity; this is echoed by the concrete paving which runs continuously from the inside onto the adjoining terrace.

Subtle but practical steps are taken to prevent garden debris from entering the house – a large coir door mat spans the width of the entrance and a boot scraper has a double function: as a door stop and as a means of removing mud from shoes.

TRANSITIONAL ROOM

The most effective way of combining the benefits of living indoors with outside pleasures is to extend your home with a conservatory, or to build a separate sun room. A transitional room could be a rustic wooden structure that is open on all sides, with climbing plants or an inexpensive solid roof forming the canopy. Even the simplest lean-to structure could create a delightful room. Alternatively, you could choose a summer house built to suit the style and proportions of your home.

Summer houses can be square, round or even octagonal; they have solid roofs and fully- or partially-glazed walls. They are usually set apart from the main building and therefore offer a different view of the outside space. They can also provide a welcome place of retreat – a quiet sanctuary where you can read, a safe place for children to play in bad weather and even a spare bedroom or work studio in summer.

Conservatories are the most luxurious of house extensions, and they should be planned and designed with sensitivity, ideally with the help of a specialist firm, if they are to integrate seamlessly with the existing style of your property. Modern technological advances have facilitated the construction of custom-made conservatories built almost entirely from glass. Most conservatories are built at ground level and cover a former patio or use the redundant space between two adjoining buildings; but successful glass rooms can also be erected on roof terraces, balconies and on the flat roofs of previous extensions.

The position and size of a conservatory may be subject to planning regulations. It is therefore advisable to consult an architect with relevant experience or a specialist company which can assess the possible options. All too often conservatories are constructed without any attention to the house's architecture. It is important to consider the size and proportions of the building, the style of windows and the colours of the brick and paintwork. It is no longer necessary to have straight small panes of glass in a conservatory, and modern metal structures even allow the use of gentle curves of glass for rounded roof shapes.

PLANTING TIPS
FOR SUN ROOMS

Frost-tender, exotic evergreen climbing
plants quickly decorate the walls and
ceilings of cool conservatories.

■ Cup and Saucer Plant
  fragrant green turning to purple
  flowers, summer; H 10-20m (30-70ft)

■ Jasmine
  fragrant pink/white flowers, late
  winter to spring; H 3m (10ft)

■ Passion-flower
  purple-pink flowers, summer to
  autumn; H 10m (30ft)

■ Morning Glory
  purple-blue flowers, spring to
  autumn; H 6m (20ft)

■ Plumbago
  sky-blue flowers, summer to
  autumn; H 3-6m (10-20ft)

■ Bougainvillaea
  white to magenta floral bracts,
  summer to autumn, H 5-8m (15-25ft)

■ Stephanotis
  fragrant, waxy, white flowers,
  spring to autumn; H 3-6m (10-20ft)

■ Glory Lily
  red/yellow flowers, summer
  to autumn; H 2m (6ft)

■ Golden Trumpet
  bright-yellow flowers, summer
  to autumn; H 5m (15ft)

SMOOTH TRANSITION

This city home was specifically designed to include a conservatory, with the result that it appears to be welded almost seamlessly to the main building. It also provides an uninterrupted view of the rear garden (far right).

Carefully thought-out details are used to make the transition from one room to another virtually unnoticeable. For instance, the yellow-painted interior wall continues outside for several feet before it reverts to the colour of the natural brick; a wall-mounted wrought-iron plant holder above the dining table contains identical geraniums to those growing outside; and the butt-jointed marble tiles in the conservatory are used singly to make stepping-stones across pale gravel to the outdoor table at the bottom of the garden.

An additional visual delight is the water feature: water is pumped up through a transparent plastic pipe that is suspended in mid-air by a shaft of clear glass, and then cascades down a metal chain into a reservoir beneath. The impact of this feature at night, when it is illuminated by concealed uplighters, is truly dramatic.

An outside room enclosed in glass could make a bright kitchen or dining room, or it could just as easily be utilized as a daylight studio or a romantic bedroom.

The function of a conservatory will largely depend on how its position relates to the rest of the house. Next to a kitchen, it's the perfect dining room – whatever the weather you can always feel as though you are dining al fresco. At night, a glass room, romantically lit by candlelight, is worth staying at home for.

Choose conservatory flooring judiciously if this room is to become a practical extension of the inside of your home. Frostproof floor tiles or paving laid in a conservatory and extended onto a terrace or patio can create a pleasing transition from one to the other, but beware of surfaces that are ultra-smooth and potentially hazardous. A plant-filled conservatory needs frequent watering and any flooring must therefore be able to withstand daily watering and the frequent traffic of muddy feet.

Conservatory furniture made from organic materials such as wood, cane or willow is hardwearing, can withstand humidity and will harmonize with any foliage. Add cushions or seat pads upholstered in neutral shades and plain fabrics to complement the natural colours of flowers and plants. These living colours will change from season to season, so avoid the chintzy, floral fabrics so often associated with conservatories, as they usually clash with the real thing; patterns like smart stripes or bold checks have much more style. Consider, too, how the conservatory's colour scheme relates to the adjoining spaces. Tones and textures in a room which is naturally lit by a window may look very different in a conservatory which is lit from above and on at least two sides.

HOT STUFF

A conservatory provides total protection from the natural elements. However, for it to be a viable living space all year round it may need cooling in summer and heating in the colder months. South-facing rooms will certainly need good ventilation – large fold-back doors, for example, or those on runners which slide open to expose an entire side, or windows and rooflights that open. Glass roofs can be fitted with automatic hydraulic windows that open when the internal temperature reaches a crucial point but remain secure. Roof blinds will filter the strongest sun, creating a comfortable shade for the people and plants beneath; they can also prevent heat loss in cooler weather. Some climbing plants may be trained on fine wires to grow just beneath a glass roof and their leaves provide a natural canopy. Grapevines, such as the variety 'Black Hamburg', are extremely fast-growing and have the additional appeal of producing edible grapes each year, provided their roots are planted outside the conservatory.

Double glazing and underfloor or perimeter heating maintain an optimum temperature in winter and are essential requirements if you intend to use the room all year round, or if you wish to cultivate tender plants and equatorial species. Some tropical varieties also need a very high level of humidity which may not be comfortable for human occupants, so desert plants might be more appropriate than those which originate from rain forests.

There are scores of familiar house plants that grow no more than an inch or so per year in most interiors but will run riot in a perennially warm conservatory. Some garden plants will behave differently in the microclimate that a conservatory provides and will grow much more prolifically than they would even a short distance away in the garden. A conservatory can provide a winter home for pot-grown tender perennials and shrubs that will live quite happily outside during the summer, giving instant natural colour to a balcony or terrace year after year. Be prepared to experiment, and try to visit public gardens that have conservatories to gain inspiration from the plants that thrive there. Remember, too, that outdoor spaces are for people – it is very easy to get carried away and buy so many plants that there is no room left for you.

GLASS MENAGERIE

For dedicated gardeners, a conservatory may replace or be an additional structure to a greenhouse. Plants can be cultivated here from seed early in the season before being transplanted to containers either in the house or out of doors once the weather is warm enough.

Some decorative plants also produce edible fruits. Varieties of tomato, for example, such as striped 'Green Zebra', purple-skinned 'Black Russian' and 'Gardener's Delight', with its superlative flavour. Fast-growing courgettes (zucchini) are grown for their edible flowers as well as for their green and yellow fruits. There is a vast range of peppers – those producing sweet and generally larger fruits as well as the plants that have tiny, fiery-flavoured cayenne and jalapeño peppers.

Herbs such as basil, parsley, chives and coriander will grow continuously in a glasshouse and can transform ordinary salads and lend a gorgeous flavour to cooked food. But they require a constant and temperate climate. These slatted and adjustable windows (left) will provide good ventilation in summer but the plants will need additional warmth in winter, which could perhaps be provided by solar panels.

INDEX

PUBLISHER'S ACKNOWLEDGMENTS

We would like to thank the following photographers/organizations for their permission to reproduce the photographs in this book:

1 Tim Griffin/Australian House & Garden (Designer: Phillip O'Malley); 2 Fritz von der Schulenburg/The Interior Archive; 3 Linda Burgess; 4-5 Alexandre Bailhache/M. Bayle/C. Puech/MCM; 6 Vivian Russell (Nichole de Vesian's garden, Bonnieu); 8-9 Alexander van Berge/Elle Wonen; 9 right Jerry Harpur; 10 left Henry Wilson/The Interior Archive (Architect: Ian Chee); 10 right Tim Beddow/The Interior Archive (Designer: Colin Childerley); 11 Jurgen Becker Fotografie (Designer:Trix Boterman); 12 Amiand Francis/Julie Borgeaud/MCM; 13 Richard Felber (Timothy Mawson); 14 Nicolas Tosi/Julie Borgeaud/MCM; 15 Marijke Heuff (Designer: A.J.van der Horst); 16 John Glover/RHS Chelsea (Designer: Christopher Bradley-Hole); 17 Christian Sarramon; 18 Tim Beddow/The Interior Archive (Designer: Colin Childerley); 19 Marie-Pierre Morel/Daniel Rozensztroch/ MCM; 20 Fritz von der Schulenburg/The Interior Archive (Architect: Nico Rensch); 21 Herbert Ypma/The Interior Archive (Architect: Javier Sordo); 22 Alexander van Berge/Elle Wonen; 23 Verne Fotografie; 24 Christian Sarramon; 25 Marie-Pierre Morel/C. Puech/MCM; 26 John Glover (Designer: Susy Smith); 27 Nicholas Kane/Arcaid (Design: Robert Sakula & Cany Ash); 28 Linda Burgess/GPL (Designer: Gilly Love); 29 Giovanna Piemonti (Architect: Antonio Anniccharico); 30 Tim Beddow/The Interior Archive (Architect: John Pawson); 31 Giles de Chabaneix/Marie Kalt/MCM (Architect: John Pawson); 32-3 Linda Burgess; 34-5 Verne Fotografie/Eigen Huis and Interieur (Designer: Kees Marcelis/stylist: Jeen Boetzel);36 Marianne Majerus (Designer: Fiona Lawrenson); 37 Mads Mogensen; 38-9 Christian Sarramon; 40 Otto Polman/Ariadne; 41 Dennis Brandsma/ VT Wonen; 42 Richard Bryant/Arcaid (Architect: Seth Stein); 43 Tim Street-Porter (Architect: Larry Totah/Vidal Sassoon's house, LA); 44 Herbert Ypma/The Interior Archive (Architect: Yturbe); 45 Cecilia Innes/The Interior Archive; 46-7 Fritz von der Schulenburg/The Interior Archive (Designer: Jasper Conran); 47 right Gilles de Chabaneix/Catherine Ardouin/MCM; 48 Herbert Ypma/The Interior Archive (Designer: Isabel Goldsmith); 49 above left Deidi von Schaewen; 49 above right John Glover/RHS Chelsea; 49 below left Christian Sarramon (Gilles St. Gilles Sol De Galets et Carreaux); 49 below right Jerry Harpur/EWA; 50 left John Glover/RHS Hampton Court (Designers: Bulatis/Fogg/Santer); 50 right Jac de Villiers/ House and Leisure Magazine; 51 left Glen Weiss/Australian House & Garden (Designer: Phillip O'Malley); 51 right Gary Rogers (Designer: Chris Moore, Napa Valley CA); 52 left Marie-Pierre Morel/Christine Puech/MCM; 52 right Alexandre Bailhache/M. Bayle/C. Puech/MCM; 53 Nicolas Tosi/Julie Borgeaud/ MCM; 54 left Mads Mogensen; 54 right Antoine Bootz/Nevis/Morsa (Designers: Antonio Morello/Donato Savoie); 55 Maria Vittoria Backhaus (Stylist: Sergio Colantuoni); 56 Fritz von der Schulenburg/The Interior Archive (Designer: Rima El-said); 57 left Mirjam Bleeker/VT Wonen; 57 right Hugh Palmer/ Pelham Cresent, London; 58 Gary Rogers (La Majorelle, Morocco, Yves St. Laurent's garden); 59 Christopher Simon Sykes/The Interior Archive (Designer: Ricciardi); 60 Marianne Majerus/RHS Chelsea (Designer: Jim Keeling/Whichford Pottery); 61 Cecilia Innes/The Interior Archive; 62 Gilles de Chabaneix/ Caroline Tine/MCM; 63 Alexander van Berge/Elle Wonen; 64-5 Reiner Blunck/Ken Done (Architect: Glen Murcutt); 65 right Christian Sarramon; 66-7 Nicola Browne/RHS Chelsea (Designer: Dan Pearson); 67 above right Richard Felber (Madison Cox's roof garden); 67 below right Herbert Ypma/The Interior Archive (Architect: Yturbe); 68 left John Glover (Designer: Susie Smith); 68-9 Hugh Palmer/Mill Valley, California; 70-1 Tim Clinch/The Interior Archive; 71 right Debbie Patterson/ Homes and Gardens/Robert Harding Syndication; 72 Jerry Harpur/ Richard Timewell; 73 Alexander van Berge/Elle Wonen; 74-5 Tim Beddow/The Interior Archive (Designer: Colin Childerley); 76 Alexander van Berge/Elle Wonen; 77 Marianne Majerus/Country Homes and Interiors/Robert Harding Syndication

AUTHOR'S ACKNOWLEDGMENTS

Many thanks to Linda Burgess, John Pawson and Kees Marcelis whose gardens we have featured; the team at Conran Octopus: Helen Fickling, Rachel Hagan and Isabel de Cordova; the tutors at the English Gardening School, especially Nada Jennett and Laura de Beden; and Sara Colledge, Ilse Oelbers and Anne Wood, who have given me their kindest support.